To

Rule
of
Thumb

A Guide to Small Business
Customer Service and Relationships

Rule of Thumb

To Steve —

Best of luck in all endeavors! And Always Make It Happen!

A Guide to Small Business Customer Service and Relationships

by

Lisa Tschauner

Lisa Tschauner

Published by

WriteLife, LLC
2323 S. 171 St.
Suite 202
Omaha, NE 68130

Rule of Thumb
3838 Davenport St
Lower Level
Omaha, NE 68131

www.writelife.com

http://ruleofthumbbiz.com

Printed in the United States of America

ISBN 978 1 60808 066 3

First Edition

Contents

Why Rule of Thumb?

Rule of Thumb: A Guide to Small Business Customer Service and Relationships is part of the Rule of Thumb series produced in affiliation with the Rule of Thumb for Business whose mission is to "enrich business growth and development." The Rule of Thumb series offers basic information in plain language that will help you start, grow and sustain your business. The explanation for using the "rule of thumb" concept was introduced in the first book and is included again here.

Throughout history, a *"Rule of Thumb"* was used in measurements in a wide variety of businesses and vocations. The following list gives a few examples of how the thumb was used for measuring:

- In agriculture, the thumb was used to measure the depth at which to plant a seed.
- In restaurants and pubs, the thumb was used to measure the temperature of beer and ale.
- Tailors used the thumb to make sure enough space was allowed between the person's skin and his/her clothing. For example, the space between the cuff of the sleeve and the wrist had to be at least the width of the thumb.
- Carpenters used the width of the thumb rather than a ruler for

measuring. For example, a notch in a board may need to be cut two thumb widths from the edge.

A "Rule of Thumb" is an idea or rule that may be applied in most situations, but not all. The "Rules of Thumb" in this book give you many reliable, convenient and simple rules that will help you remember many "dos" and "don'ts" that go with owning and running a business.

Introduction
The Power of Customer Service

In the early eighties, there was a shy teenage boy named Sam. Sam lived in a large metropolitan city, and he did all of the normal things that teenage boys did. He played video games, watched MTV, was active is school sports and hung out with his friends. However, one thing that set Sam apart was that he had a love of old sports cars. Most kids in the city didn't even think about getting a car until they went to college or moved out of the city. Influenced by a family friend, Sam had the desire to purchase an old muscle car and fix it up. He approached his parents and they told him that they would help him pursue this, but that he would have to come up with half of the money.

This meant that Sam would need a job. He feverishly hit the streets filling out many job applications, but he struck out because many businesses wouldn't hire kids under the age of sixteen. Then his uncle told him he could work in his convenience store after school stocking shelves, cleaning and sometimes helping customers. Sam was very excited about this. He was going to actually earn money at the age of fifteen and would be able to purchase the vehicle he wanted; hopefully by the time he turned sixteen.

Sam started his job the next week and quickly learned the daily operation. Cleaning and stocking inventory were pretty easy as Sam was an organized person for his age. He did well, and it wasn't long before his uncle allowed him to work directly with the customers. At first, he was very shy. He knew that he just needed to be brave and try helping people. One day, he noticed an older gentleman standing in an isle looking at a display of gloves, hats and umbrellas. He walked out from behind the counter and asked the man if he could help him find something. The old man grumbled and simply stated that there wasn't anything he could do and he was useless. This really struck Sam. This was one of his first real attempts at helping a customer and he wondered what he had done wrong. Sam tried to ask the man what he was looking for but, it didn't help. He just barked at Sam that they didn't have the ice scrapers he needed. He said that he would just go to another store and never come back. Sam looked around at the store. He hoped that his uncle wasn't watching.

After the man walked out of the store, Sam went back behind the counter and replayed the situation over and over in his mind. He didn't understand why this man was so upset with him. He thought maybe he startled the man, maybe he looked too young, or maybe he forgot to smile. His uncle told him to always smile. He just couldn't figure it out. He went through the rest of the day in a state of shock and wonder.

A few days later, he decided to give it another try. There was a lady looking at a round rack of postcards. He straightened out

*his apron and walked over to her. He remembered to smile and use
a very nice voice and look her in the eyes. He offered to help her
find what she wanted. She smiled and proclaimed what a nice young
gentleman he was. She started taking several cards from the rack.
She stated that she really needed some postcards with pictures of the
local fountain on them, but it was okay. She could use the ones they
had. She started small talk and asked Sam how he was and they had
a great conversation. He apologized for not having postcards like
she wanted, but she just shook her head and told him it wasn't a big
deal. She said that it wasn't the end of the world. She paid for her
purchase and told Sam that he was delightful and it was very nice to
meet him. After she left the store, Sam actually started to smile and
giggle a bit. He felt really good inside and was in a great mood the
rest of the day. He went home that evening feeling really good about
the job he had done. He even stayed a few minutes late to make sure
all of the shelves were stocked and faced for the next day.*

*As Sam continued on with this job, he realized something pivotal.
Aside from the occasional grumpy customer and the occasional
happy-go-lucky customer, most customers were pretty neutral about
their transactions. He started to get more comfortable talking
with customers, asking questions and getting to know them better.
When he did this, he realized suddenly they looked directly at him
rather than in their wallets or across the shelves. They smiled back
and they started to get to know him. He became more confident
and realized in most cases, he could steer the interaction with the
customer.*

Sam continued to work for his Uncle while in high school. He got very good at his job and often thought a lot about these first customers of his. He eventually saved his money, bought his car and went to college. In college, he worked several jobs that required him to interact with customers. He worked in a grocery store, a restaurant, and a store that sold outdoor recreation equipment. After college, he got a job as an auto mechanic and eventually purchased this business. He expanded it to include a service station as well as the repair shop.

Throughout all of his work experiences, he was very interested in how he interacted with customers. He started to track the demeanor of his customers. What he found was that approximately 10% of customers were NEVER satisfied; similar to the first old man in his Uncle's convenience store. Then he discovered that about 10% of customers are just nice and happy regardless of whether he was able to meet their needs or are able to solve their problems. They are just friendly like the lady shopping for postcards. Together, that made up about 20% of the customer base, leaving 80%. This was what was most interesting to Sam. He knew that no matter what he did; he was not able to control the 20% of people who were inevitably difficult or overly happy. They were simply on opposite ends of the spectrum and he couldn't spend the time to change their personalities. However, what Sam did discovered was that the remaining 80% responded to him in the same way that he treated them. If Sam was short and didn't smile, neither did the customer. If Sam smiled and said "hello" and was friendly, so was the customer.

If Sam showed appreciation toward the customer, they did the same to him.

Chart of Influence

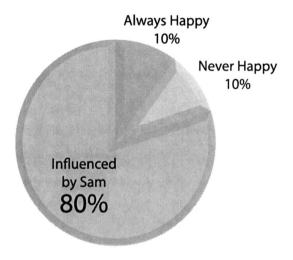

What really impacted Sam the most was watching his customers as they interacted with each other after Sam had approached them and helped them. They tended to treat others the way they had just been treated. Sam realized after several years of working with customers that he had an incredible power. Of all the people he came in contact with, he was able to control the way that 80% of them would residually treat other people that they interacted with, including him. He was humbled by this responsibility, but soon used it to his advantage. He realized that if he could learn to build a foundation of courtesy, helpfulness and respect he was way ahead of the game. The best part of this tool was that Sam was positively affecting the people around him. He was making them feel good

*inside and creating an environment that made it possible for others
to benefit from this.*

*Sam was able to use this knowledge and perfect his approach to
customer service. He was able to hire employees and train them in a
way that allowed them to use this same tool. He was very successful
in what he did and he lived a very good life as he was active in
his community and considered a leader. Sam often reflects back
on his younger days as a shy, teenage boy working in his uncle's
convenience store. He realized that because of perceiving customer
service as a learning opportunity he was able to model his future
jobs and business into one with high-quality customer service. It led
to many customers "wanting" to do business with Sam and feeling
good about it.*

This book is focused on customer service basics with some
of the new management styles and industry trends we are seeing
in today's business world integrated throughout. My hope is that
you can use this book as a catalyst in developing your customer
service platform. I have worked with many business owners and I
always ask them what they feel the most important aspect is to being
successful in their business. The majority have responded by saying
that CUSTOMER SERVICE is the key element to success. I find it
strange that when I visit the book store (I actually did this recently)
and ask where the section is on customer service, they take me to a
small group of books (10-15) at the end of the business, marketing
or management section. We need to share our best practices and
information that we have learned about customer service and that is

why I have always considered this a passion.

As entrepreneurs build their businesses, it is easy for them to be consumed by the daily tasks and operation of the business and over-look customers. Without the customer, the bank does not grow. The livelihood of your business is ultimately in the hands of your customer. Take the time to discover a way to implement remarkable customer service practices into what you do in your business. Some of what you read in this book may be new ideas or tactics, but much of it is a reminder of things you know, but maybe haven't thought about in a while. When you consider your customers first and base your business decisions around that concept, you will be surprised at the difference it can make in your business. When you are willing to create a memorable and positive experience for your customers they will find value in this. Customers will feel good about doing business with you and this will create a unique culture for your business. Making money is always a goal for a business, but if you decide to create value for your customers first, increasing your bottom line will be a welcome outcome.

Chapter 1
What is a Customer?

Definition

We have all been customers and we have all worked with customers. Sometimes, we may not even know when we are interacting with a person who should be considered a customer. Each business probably has an idea about who their customers are. They understand what groups of people find their products and services appealing. However, is this description one that would satisfy every business? Many experts have defined what a customer is. We can look at what the dictionary tells us:

- *A party that receives or consumes products (goods or services) and has the ability to choose between different products and suppliers* (www.businessdictionary.com), or

- *A person who purchases goods or services from another; buyer; patron.* (www.dictionary.com), or

- *A person who buys; A person whom one has dealings.*

  (Collins English Dictionary, 2009)

 Rule of Thumb:
Each business owner needs to define what a customer is to their business.

This is a critical process in order to be sure you are reaching your customers and communicating with them as necessary. One strategy to do that would be to ask:

1. Is the person that stops into my business to make a one-time purchase considered a customer?

2. Is the mailman who brings in the daily correspondence considered a customer?

3. Is my neighbor who hasn't ever entered my establishment considered a customer?

Yes, Yes and Yes. In each of these situations, the person on the opposite side is a customer whether he or she is a new, referring, or potential customer. The first question is easy – sure even though it is a one-time purchase, that person is considered a customer. However, the mailman – he hasn't ever bought anything, but is it possible to still consider him a customer? Is it only fair to consider a person a customer at the point that money exchanges hands and the contract is complete? He comes in every day; you smile, take the mail, and exchange small talk about the weather and last night's high school basketball game because you both have kids in high school. Then months later, he needs a widget similar to the ones that you sell in your business. He considers shopping online to purchase the widget but then remembers that you sell widgets too. If he feels like a customer, do you think he will be more inclined to purchase that widget from you? How can you make him a customer before he even considers becoming one?

What about the third scenario? Your neighbor is a retired school teacher. He isn't even interested in widgeting, but he knows that you own a business for widgetors. When he is at the local coffee shop for his weekly gathering of other retirees, he hears one of them share that his son is in the market for a new widget. He then pipes up and with a proud face tells them all about your business and what a great person you are. He has instantly taken over the role of "salesman" because of his loyalty as your neighbor and the feeling he has which is that similar to a customer. What did you do to make him feel like a valued customer knowing that he will never make a widget purchase?

When trying to determine the definition of a customer; I prefer the simple definition from the Merriam-Webster dictionary: an individual usually having some specified distinctive trait. With this definition in mind, is it possible to help form that distinctive trait in each person you know and even those you have yet to meet? The distinctive trait is that each person or customer is a promoter of your business, whether he or she is someone who actually makes purchases or someone who tells everyone about your business and the experience you offer. Although this is a shift in the perception of what a customer may be, it would certainly open our minds and grow our customer lists! So now, instead of showing customer appreciation only to those who actually buy from us, we get to expand our customer base by transforming all of those who are in our "sphere of influence" into what we consider customers!

The root of the word customer is "custom" which means habit, way of acting, established practice, account, guest, collective pattern, behavior and established activity. Focus on encouraging habits or practices that will raise awareness and get people talking about your business. Promote this with your customers while pursuing new customers and maintaining relationships with current customers. It will benefit the business and create a positive buzz.

Rule of Thumb:
People dedicated to promoting your business whenever possible is going to benefit you and your bottom line!

Target customers

Now that we have determined that everyone in your contact list has the potential to impact your business and your customer base, you need to start categorizing your customers in terms of your products and services. This is what we call defining your target market. Although we need to treat everyone as our customer, where we spend our advertising budget and how we grow our offerings is dependent on the primary customer, secondary customer and so forth. This process is a necessity for a business owner. You must have the goal of reaching the people who will ideally benefit from your product or service. This is done by communicating and marketing your message directly to them. This is the first step to having an effective marketing campaign. Everyone wants to appeal to the masses, but what results is a mediocre level of service and goods. Correlate this with the saying,

> **Rule of Thumb:**
> "It is better to be GREAT at one thing than just GOOD at many things."

Determining your primary customer will allow you to meet their needs and be that GREAT choice for them.

Primary Customer – This is the person <u>most likely</u> to use your product or service with the most frequency and creating the greatest profit. Be specific. Sure, your customer may range in age from 18-65, but the most frequent customer falls between the ages of 31-46. Consider a local restaurant in a middle-class neighborhood; their customers range in age, but which customers can they count on as repeat customers and to spend the most amount of money? It is nice to have the older, retired community as customers, but they rarely order drinks from the bar and they tend to be more conservative altogether. The teenagers are frequent customers that tend purchase the lower-cost items like appetizers and soft drinks. The primary market for the restaurant is the young families that come with several children and friends who want to relax for an hour or two while they eat, drink and enjoy the atmosphere. Therefore, 80% of all marketing messages need to be directed at this group of people.

Try to identify this segment with specific information in these areas; geographics, demographics and psychographics. Know the following things about your primary customer:

Geographic Information

Where is your customer located?

Area (region, state, city)	
Population (urban, suburban, rural)	
Type of location (commercial, residential, recreational)	
Climate and Seasonal Information	
Industry or Agricultural Focus	
Recreational Opportunities	

Demographic Information

What are the details about your customer? If your business is geared toward reaching the end user; business-to-customer (B2C), then identify these specifics for your customer. If your business is focused on business-to-business (B2B), then identify the information on the business side.

Consumer		Business	
Age Range		Industry	
Income Range		Sector	
Gender		Length of time in Business	
Occupation		Company Revenues	
Marital Status		Number of Employees	
Family-Size		Number of Locations	
Ethnicity		Size of Location	
Education Level		Company Owner	
Homeowner or Renter		Other	
Other			

Psychographics

Think about your primary customer and what they value. What are their goals, mission and motivational drivers? Use your best judgment as you select the important factors about your target customer. This will help you create a marketing campaign that delivers a message that will have impact.

 Rule of Thumb:
Your goal is to be effective in where you spend your advertising dollars by creating an influence on your customers.

Knowing the psychographics of your customer will also be one of the first steps you can take to "getting to know them."

Consumer	Business
Technology Focused	Technology Focused
Status is Important	Business Leader
Trend-Setting	Innovative
Socially Responsible	Socially Responsible
Family-Oriented	Financial Market
Likes to have fun	Industry Leader
Environmentally Aware	Agricultural
Conservative	Food/Entertainment
Responsible	Business to Business
Fashionable	Business to Consumer
Other _____	Other _____
Other _____	Other _____

Be specific, and try to narrow this focus as much as possible. We tend to group families, businesses and other groups who are interested or have a use for the products and services we sell. Keep in mind that as you determine your primary customers, you should gear this for the actual decision maker.

The value of a customer

Examining the value placed on a customer, especially when we consider the wide spectrum of customers, can be a very subjective activity. It is difficult to determine the residual effects of a customer who is always recommending your business to others or who references your website in their blog. Many times, you are not even aware of the value a customer may carry because you are not knowledgeable about all they do to promote your business. If you are a "numbers" person and still wish to place a value or rating to each of your customers, I encourage you to do this. Your accountant will also be impressed! There are many different approaches to evaluating the value of a customer based on money, but these practices are fairly in-depth.

Repeat Customers and New Customers –A repeat customer is someone who does business more than once, and a new customer is doing business for the first time with your company. Which one is more important? There are many different theories on this topic and it is dependent on the type of business being addressed. However, I will share this perspective from Doug Bruce, the owner of Bruce Furniture in Nebraska: "Our goal is not to get new customers, but to create happy customers. We are problem solvers for our customers and when they are happy, the rest falls into place." Based on this outlook, new customers will be generated as a result of keeping existing customers happy.

Rule of Thumb:
Now for the challenge; instill the sense of customer in everyone you meet regardless of the reason for the encounter.

The lesson in this chapter is to treat everyone you know and meet as a potential customer, but be well aware of your actual target customer and focus your main marketing messages toward that collective. You will impact your target, and in this process you will also create awareness with your secondary and tertiary markets. Know the value of your existing customers and focus on making them happy as it will naturally grow your customer base.

Chapter 2
Why do Customers do Business?

<u>Understanding customer psychology</u>

Rule of Thumb:
Customers have choices.

This is something that every business owner must accept and recognize as an opportunity. All customers have the choice of where they do business and which businesses they promote. As a business owner, it is your opportunity to become the choice of your customer. In order to be their first choice, you must first understand what motivates your customers. We can look at the obvious drivers: price, quality, convenience, uniqueness, and trends. However, all of these things are actually symptoms of a deeper motivational driver. Let's examine why we are influenced by these things:

Price: We want to spend as little as possible and get as much or the best that we can because we then have more money to spend on other things that we want. When we are given a fair or great price or an exceptional deal, we see it as value and it makes us *feel good* about the transaction.

Quality: We know the difference between good and bad quality. We want to invest our money into purchases that will last and bring us expected results. When we get expected results and beyond, we *feel good* knowing we made a great decision.

Convenience: We are busy people. We want things that will help us multi-task and make life a bit easier. It would be counter-productive to purchase products and services that are difficult to use or make our lives more hectic. When we are able to streamline something that we do and be more efficient in our daily activities, we are on top of our game and *feel good*.

Uniqueness: When we are able to have something first or have a one-of-a-kind product or service, it makes us feel privileged and special. We often brag about or showcase these types of purchases because we are proud and want to let others know about the unique thing we have. We *feel good* when someone else is in awe of something we have, and it makes us *feel good* to have the attention.

Trends: We have a natural inclination to replicate those around us and "keep up with the Joneses" so we are very likely to want the same trendy items and opportunities that our friends, families and peers have. When we have these trendy things, we feel like we belong and are equal to those around us. Having the same things as others and the "cool" things out there gives us a sense of security and fills a satisfaction that makes us *feel good*.

After examining our motivators, is that deeper need we have to fulfill for our customers obvious? We want to *feel good* about ourselves. We want to feel like we are cool, smart, envied, and accepted.

Rule of Thumb:
Customers have the need to feel good about themselves.

Think back to Psychology 101 and Abraham Maslow's hierarchy of needs.

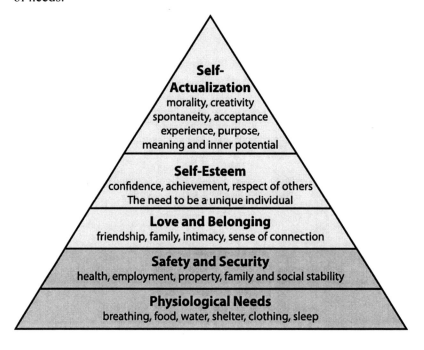

At the top of that list are Self-Esteem and Self-Actualization. We are always trying to reach these after we satisfy the first three levels. As a business owners we often offer the products and services that are necessary for the basic needs found in the first two levels. If we can meet those needs and also bring value to the customer that delivers on the top three levels, will we leave our customers feeling fulfilled and most importantly, feeling good about themselves. Something special happens when we deliver on those top level needs. We are wired to know that when we like the results we get from something, we tend to do it again and again. In consistently delivering that top-level service, we are creating that "custom" or habit in our customer.

This is easy to understand. When we don't enjoy or feel good about something, we avoid it.

> **Rule of Thumb:**
> When we feel good and happy about something, we are drawn to it.

We must recognize that this principle applies to our customers. In most cases, they have that same desire that we have. So the challenge – or rather the opportunity – is to make the customer feel good about themselves and the transaction. This can be accomplished by not only giving them the products and services, but more importantly, making the experience valuable to them. If the process is something that gives them a good feeling, they will like it. The price, quality, convenience, uniqueness and trends are the first step and will get the customers to you and to offer consideration. But, now we know that we can do so much more to make a customer feel pleased and content.

Consider this example:

I ordered some photo prints online and selected the option to pick them up at a local big-chain retailer's photo lab. I spent over $70.00 on these prints of various sizes. I had requested all matte finishing on the prints, but when I picked them up they were not printed correctly. I took them back to the store and learned that the online ordering system allows many options that aren't always available in the local retail photo labs. I ended up returning most of the photos and getting a credit. Typically this would be a frustrating experience, and I would leave not feeling good about the transaction. However, the photo lab technician and store manager were both so nice and concerned about my issues that I was unexpectedly satisfied with the experience. The manager told me he would happily refund my money but that it was more important to him that I was happy with my prints. He invited me back into the lab to choose the pictures I wanted reprinted directly from the screen. I was amazed and felt very "valued" considering the error was not all their fault. I made two trips and spent more than an hour on this purchase. Ironically, I left the store with a happy and good feeling. I was more informed about the process of ordering my prints and how to do it properly. I know that I will return to this photo lab to order my prints and probably many future orders. I felt awesome, and this was certainly a great experience for me.

Meeting the customers' needs
and fulfilling the customers' wants

Rule of Thumb:
To meet customers' needs and fulfill their wants, take a look at the perks your business offers.

Let's say you sell used cars and are located in a city that hosts two colleges and four large high schools. You have identified that your target market is high school and college students.

Let's look at what your customer needs:

1. Transportation to and from work and school and occasionally out of town when college students go home.

2. A car payment that fits in the budget of a college student

3. Good gas mileage

How about the wants:

1. Great stereo system

2. Comfortable and stylish

3. Electric windows

4. Keyless entry

5. Navigation

6. Heated seats

If you can give the customer a vehicle that meets their needs and also fulfills some of these wants, you will tap into that subconscious feeling of satisfaction. The customer knows they need a vehicle that works, gets good gas mileage and has low payment. Therefore, finding a car that meets these requirements makes them feel that they accomplished a task. However, when they also get a high-tech stereo system, keyless entry and heated seats they will "feel good" about themselves because of the pleasure and value they find in these other features. Learning about what your customer wants in addition to what they need is all done through communication which we will discuss in chapter three.

Observe and learn

I believe in learning from experiences.

Rule of Thumb:
Take the time to observe other customer service situations and learn from them.

As you watch and learn, you can identify best practices that you witness and adapt them to how you interact with customers in your business. On the next page is a form that you can use to guide you through this process.

Critique of Customer Service Experience

Name of Business: _____

Date of Visit: _____ Time of Visit: _____

1) What was the purpose of your visit?
    Buying Something Needed
    Buying Something Wanted
    Taking Care of Daily Business (Bank, Insurance, Dentist...etc.)
    Seeking Service (Making appointment, oil change...etc.)
    Resolving a Problem
    Other: _____

2) Did you feel welcomed?
    YES   NO

3) Were you acknowledged?
    YES   NO

4) Did someone offer to help you? Please explain.
    YES   NO
Explain:_____

5) If yes, did they smile and/or shake your hand?
    YES   NO

6) Describe your mood: (mark all that apply)

    Annoyed   Rushed
    Neutral   Calm
    Cheerful   Assertive
    Passive   Friendly
    Aloof   Angry
    Other: _____

Do you consider this visit a success? Explain.
    YES   NO
Explain:_____

8) What could the business representative done differently:
_____
_____
_____
_____

9) What did the business representative do well:
_____
_____
_____
_____

10) Other comments to describe your experience:
_____
_____

11) On a scale from 1 to 10 with 10 being the best, how would you rate this experience? _____

The paramount message found in this chapter is that customers act based on what they need, but they are driven by what they want both consciously and subconsciously. Working on your customer service strategy with the goal of making your customers feel good about themselves and the choices they make will lead to customer satisfaction.

Chapter 3
Communicating with Customers

Getting to know your customers

Now that you have identified your target customers, you can also identify the best way to reach them and actively communicate with them. This may be through networking, email, mobile marketing or even calling them on the phone. It's important that you make the communication easy for your customer. If your target customer is the baby boomer demographic, chances are that texting information to them about your business will not be very effective.

 Rule of Thumb:
The best way to know how to communicate is to ask.

Also, be informed about what is happening around you and in your community. If a specific event is happening that will attract many of your customers, try to become a part of that event. If there is a new software program that many of your customers are using, learn more about it so that you can visit with them about it. If one of your customers has recently been recognized for something in the community, know about this and be prepared to acknowledge them.

In most cases, as indicated in the introduction, you have the ability to control the interaction you have with your customers. Three very important factors to consider when you set out to control the opportunity to communicate include: Smile, Information, and Value.

SMILE – This is the ultimate tool. How often do you seriously think about your smile? Be sure that when you encounter (even over the phone or through email) your customer you are smiling. This comes through ALWAYS! It creates a friendly and comfortable situation and relieves tension that may be there. When you smile at someone, the typical response is for them to smile back. This will create an immediate positive and friendly impression. It also puts both parties at ease, and makes it easier to communicate.

INFORMATION – Be sure that when you speak to a customer about your business, you are prepared to give them useful information. Know when to keep it simple and know when to give them in-depth details. Tell them what to expect and facts to consider as they continue shopping. Don't keep helpful information from a consumer because you fear that it may help them make a purchase elsewhere. When you give them helpful and thoughtful information, they will develop respect for you. They will appreciate your honesty and it also shows them that you are confident in your product and service. You truly can't go wrong by looking out for the best interest of your customer. Regardless of the outcome, you will feel positive about this opportunity. Customers will view you as the expert and in most cases will return because you offered the most accurate and useful information.

VALUE – Find value in everyone. When you interact with your customer, it is your time to let them know that your product, service, ideas, and methods are valuable to them. However, be sure that you are tapping into that their subconscious need to be important and appreciated. Acknowledge their questions as being relevant. Compliment them on bringing up important concerns and issues. This will help validate their efforts.

Rule of Thumb:
Let each customer know that you value what they bring to you as well.

This will make them feel a sense of pride and create that "feel good" mentality we want to encourage.

Imagine this situation with a customer:

BUSINESS: *Thank you so much for calling us at Ken's Computer Service. How can I help you?*

CUSTOMER: *Well, I need to have a virus protection program installed on my laptop.*

BUSINESS: *I am glad you called. At Ken's, we offer several programs that could meet your needs. Can you tell me what you do with your computer?*

CUSTOMER: *I am a photographer, so I want to be sure that I am able to store large photo files and also upload them onto the Internet so that my customers can view them.*

BUSINESS: *<u>Thank you for letting me know this.</u> Our FileSafe program would be very good for your application. You can access your files on your computer, upload them and share them without jeopardizing your client's privacy. <u>As a business owner, I am sure this is important to you, right?</u>*

CUSTOMER: *Sure. How much does it cost?*

BUSINESS: *<u>Great question.</u> We offer this program for the suggested retail price of $99.00. However, we include installation at no additional charge. <u>We know how important your time is.</u> You want to be able to do what you do best which is take great photos for your clients, so <u>we want to take care of this for you.</u>*

CUSTOMER: *Okay, great. When can you do this?*

BUSINESS: *Our hours are M-F, 10:00 am – 5:30 pm. This service will take about an hour. <u>Your schedule is just as important, so tell me what time it would work for you?</u>*

CUSTOMER: *Friday, at noon.*

BUSINESS: *Great. Just bring in your laptop and we will take care of everything. We want to let you know that <u>we really appreciate that you called us today.</u> We will do what we can to give you the best product and service and save you time and money. <u>Does that make a difference for you?</u>*

CUSTOMER: *Uh, (customer takes a moment because nobody has ever asked this before) yes, it sure does make a difference. Thank you.*

BUSINESS: *Is there anything else that we can do to make this process easier or better for you?*

CUSTOMER: *(pinches himself) No, this is great…wait, where are you located?*

BUSINESS: *Oh, thanks for reminding me to share that with you. We are in the strip mall east of town, next to the cable company. Give me your email and I can send you a link with the address, map, and directions. There are also several restaurants and food vendors nearby since you are coming around lunch time.*

CUSTOMER: *GREAT!*

BUSINESS: *Well, thank you and we will see you on Friday.*

In this scenario, there are several opportunities (<u>underlined</u>) where the business representative shows how much he values the customer. He does this by "guiding" or helping the direction of the service call. Imagine how the customer feels when he hangs up the phone!

Asking the right questions

To learn more about our customers' needs and wants, we must be sure we are asking the right questions and for the right reasons.

Rule of Thumb:
As humans, we ask questions in order to reduce our level of uncertainty.

According the Uncertainty Reduction Theory (Berger & Calabrese, 1975) we ask questions because we can anticipate what will happen when we are less uncertain. As you develop your customer communication strategies ask questions that will provide clarification, purpose, relevance, accuracy and evaluation.

Clarification - Can you tell me more about that? What exactly do you mean?

Purpose - Why would you like that? What do you want to accomplish?

Relevance - How does that work? Can you explain that process? How will this meet your expectations?

Accuracy - Can you give me an example? Is there anything I have missed? Can you describe this?

Evaluation - What are the pros and cons? How much is that worth to you? How do you make decisions?

The next step to asking questions successfully is **LISTENING**. You must really listen to what your customer is telling you in response to these questions. They will want to see how you meet their needs while being aware of what they have told you. Think about how disheartening it is for you when you spend time explaining something to someone to find out that they didn't remember or even think that what you said was important. Don't leave your customers with that same feeling.

Rule of Thumb:
Listening well will let your customer know how much you value them and what they say.

Relating to your customer's world

We have a tendency to talk our talk and assume that everyone knows what we are saying. Have you ever been the customer in this situation? A good example is when you call an insurance company in response to an Explanation of Benefits statement and they begin speaking to you using their lingo, abbreviations, and acronyms. Pretty soon you feel like you need to get off the phone, research this information through a get a secret decoder ring, or find a translator, and then call back and perhaps feel the same way. It can be very intimidating and very frustrating. Remember you don't want your customers to feel this way.

Rule of Thumb:
Talk to your customers with language that they will understand.

This is an opportunity to fine tune those communication skills. You must look at each customer on an individualized basis. Consider what they do for a living, how they spend their leisure time, what their education level is and be prepared to explain your service and business in a way that applies to their world. They will understand much better and will appreciate this approach. They will also be able to evaluate what you are saying based on how you positioned the information to relate to their specific situation and within the context of their environment.

For instance, if you are talking to a customer who just purchased a vacation package, be sure to not just use lingo that is specific to the travel industry. Instead of saying: *"you will need a voucher during peak to pay less than rack rate. You can pick this up at the CVB upon arrival"*

Maybe rephrase this to: *"Since you and your family are traveling during the most popular time of year for your vacation, you still have the opportunity to save money. When you arrive, you can contact the local visitor's bureau to get a voucher, similar to a coupon. This will give you a discount and allow you to pay less than the price that everyone else has to pay."*

First impressions

How many times have you visited a business or company and felt that the first impression was lacking something?

Rule of Thumb:
The first impression is very important as it is an excellent and exclusive opportunity to set the tone with a customer.

Acknowledging a customer immediately is critical to setting the right first impression. This doesn't mean that you have to smother or be "overly friendly" with your customers, but you do need to give them attention.

Shake it up when you try to serve their needs. Instead of approaching them in a predictable way, surprise them. Attempt a fresh approach so they cannot anticipate your first encounter. This will pique their curiosity and may create an engaging situation where you will get to know them better.

For instance, 75% of the responses to the typical customer service greeting we are all used to, "May I help you?" will be, "No, I am just looking." So, why not ask a different question that will open up an opportunity for dialogue. Maybe consider: "Is this the first time you've been in our store?" or "Can I tell you about our specials?" When you do this, you get to open up the two-way path of conversation.

Another way to break the ice is to compliment the customer. You can't fake this. It must be genuine regardless of how slight. So, use the Thumper Theory – if you can't say anything nice, don't say anything at all. In most cases, you can find a compliment to deliver to a customer. It can be very simple; EXAMPLE – "Oh, what a cute purse. Where did you get that?" Or the compliment can be more rational. EXAMPLE – "I like your idea to bundle those services. I really appreciate the suggestion." However you choose to acknowledge your customer, try to compliment them in a positive and genuine way.

Serving the "well-informed" customer

In the age of technology and information availability, customers are more knowledgeable than ever before.

 Rule of Thumb:
Customer service has changed because of the amount and accessibility of information available.

Often our customers are getting information that even we don't have. The majority of people walk around with computers in their pockets, so having access to instant data is not a barrier. Customers have gotten into the habit of checking online before they do anything else. They can get information about features and benefits, warranties, product support, prices and one of the most important things; reviews from other customers and industry experts.

For example, I purchased a mini-projector for my computer about a year ago. I had wanted to get one to make presentations on the road much easier. Knowing that I wanted one of these techno-gadgets, I had been researching for probably about two years – really. I even had a special favorites folder in my browser to keep links to some of the product and industry information that I found to be helpful. Although I love the ease of online purchasing and the reinforcement of product reviews, this purchase was still significant enough that I actually wanted to see the product. When it came time to make the purchase, I knew EXACTLY what I wanted. I had even checked online with the local big-box store so that I could see if they had the one I wanted in stock. When I walked into the store to buy this, I was immediately acknowledged and helped. The salesman wanted to tell me all about these projectors and show me the selection that they had to offer. When I explained to him the process I had went through and that I knew what I wanted and that I already knew they even had it in stock, he seemed a bit taken aback. In fact, he seemed almost disappointed that he didn't get to "sell" me on a projector.

When you are faced with a customer that has been educated online about the products and services that your business offers, you must be open-minded and accept that this is the world today. Let the customer know that you are impressed with the due diligence they have taken to learn about what they want. Ask them what information they did find, and if they have questions about your business based on what they have researched. Often customers spend hours and even days looking and reading online before actually shopping. It is important that you acknowledge the time and effort that they have put into this.

It is still important to try to know as much as possible and make it a goal to know more than anyone else about your product or service, but you have to be realistic. There is an overload of information available to consumers. Look at this as an opportunity to focus your efforts on creating more of an experience for the customer. Instead of spending your time selling them on the features and benefits of a product that they already know they want, GIVE IT TO THEM. Close the deal and spend the extra time on building a great relationship. Learn more about them so that you can make them feel great about the purchase they have made. When you start working with a customer, ask them what they know and where they have gotten the information. This lets you know from the start how to approach the customer service experience. Think of it as an advantage that much of the facts are online and that customers can make an educated decision based on that if they choose.

Also, take the time to be as knowledgeable as you can be about what information is out there about your industry. This will help you be familiar with the same sites and data portals that your customers are accessing so that you can be better prepared when they share this information with you.

Dealing with customer issues

Smile, Smile, Smile and then Smile again. I cannot stress the importance of this enough. If a customer contacts you with a product issue or maybe because they are unhappy with the service of your business, you have to keep in mind that you have 80% of the control in this situation.

Rule of Thumb:
You can start by smiling which in most all situations will create a friendly and less-hostile environment.

Your tone will come through even over the phone and through email, so make it pleasant. Approaching a customer issue this way will show that you are open to finding a solution. If you frown or grumble to them, they will immediately be defensive which is not ideal for effective communication. You want this experience to be positive. Keep this situation calm, controlled and look at it as a chance to relate to your customer from a different angle.

Rule of Thumb:
Have an open mind about customer concerns, complaints and issues.

Consider it from the perspective that customers who take the time to complain are not attacking or insulting you, they are giving you a second chance to get it right. This shows that they are very willing and interested in doing business with you. Don't take it personally! At this point, the issue is not going to disappear so how you respond to it is how your customer will judge you and your business.

Step 1 – Listen

Allow yourself to truly listen to what your customer is saying and to listen to everything they are saying. This will allow you to analyze what he is saying before you respond. This also enables you to make an intelligent recommendation to solve his problem. Be sure to ask relevant questions if you need more information to make a qualified response.

Step 2 – Recognize and empathize with the customer's feelings

When you do switch paradigms to see a situation from your customer's perspective, this allows you to validate how they feel. Relate to their feelings. Ask yourself how you would really feel and why. You will gain understanding and create a situation that will foster recovery or remedy.

Step 3 – Sometimes an apology is the solution

Two very powerful words – "I'm Sorry." When someone

hears this, their defensive barrier often immediately crumbles. You are also validating their feelings by offering an apology. Consider this response – "I'm sorry that this happened. Please, tell me how I can fix this and make it better." Saying you are sorry is not an omission of guilt. That often seems to be the belief and the reason that many people forego an apology. Keep in mind that you want your customer happy, so simply saying that you are sorry they feel unsatisfied is very justified on your part. It can be the first step to moving forward.

Step 4 – Thank the customer for bringing the problem to your attention

Again, this shows that you value the opinion of your customer. It makes them feel that you are open-minded and are always looking for ways that you can improve your business. This is considered a step toward progress. Customers want to know that the businesses they deal with are always progressing. This also gives the customers a sense of how much you value your business. Remember, you are in control of setting that bar.

Step 5 – Explain what you are going to do

DO NOT IGNORE a concern or issue a customer brings to your attention. It will not go away. If you ignore a customer issue, it might seem to disappear, but it will never go away. The problem or concerns always remain in the customer's mind and will affect their future business decisions. Explain to the customer your plan to remedy the situation and be sure to execute. If the situation allows for it, contact the customer after you have done what you committed to do. Your follow-through shows the customer you are responsible and proves they can rely on you.

Effective communication is the key to success. Take the time to get to know your customers and build rapport with them. Make it easy for your customers to get information from you and make that information valuable. Ask the right questions that will allow you to really understand what your customer needs and what they want. Listen, listen and listen. First impressions are an opportunity. Deal head-on with customer issues and respond to them in the best way possible. This is the only "right" way to do it.

Chapter 4
Where does Customer Service Exist?

Not only in your business and during hours of operation

Imagine you are at the post office to pick up your mail from your post office box. There is a slip inside telling you that you have a package too large to put into the box, and you will have to retrieve it at the counter. You take your place in line with the other customers waiting to speak with a post office representative. You notice that the owner of the hair salon where you get your hair done is next in line. She is always so friendly and helpful when you are at the salon. Sometimes she even offers you a cold soda and brings magazines to you while your hair is drying. She doesn't notice you. There are several people standing between you, so you decide to just wait to say hello.

When she steps up to the counter, the clerk greets her. She immediately slaps down a pile of envelopes on the counter and begins to raise her voice to the post office clerk. She is complaining because the letters she sent were returned due to insufficient addresses. She was demanding that the post office allow her to send these to the correct addresses at no charge. She is using a very harsh tone and has a rude disposition. The clerk explains that they cannot do this because this mistake was not due to an error on their part.

However, he is able to sell her pre-printed postage envelopes for the same price as a stamp so she could correctly address and send her letters immediately without making a separate trip. She gets very irate with the clerk and even insults him. In this situation, you see a different side to this business owner. Would your opinion of her change? Would you have a difficult time over-looking this situation when you have the opportunity to interact or patron her business again?

Keep this in mind as you are outside of your business and technically "off work." In small communities, chances are that you will bump into someone who knows you and perhaps even a customer or two. Others will form an impression about you based on how you conduct yourself and treat other people. Just remember that customer service is a mindset and not just an act you put on when working with customers in your business. Make it a practice to simply be nice and to treat others with respect as well as listen to their needs and wants. If you can make this part of your daily approach in all things you are involved with, eventually you will create a positive reputation as a business owner and about your business. You will be a productive leader in your community and for other businesses because, over time, your positive attitude will begin to affect how others conduct themselves as well.

Business relationships

We don't live on an island and we can't do everything by ourselves. Each day we work with other people to make the things happen in our business. These people may be our neighboring businesses, our office supply sales representative, the teller at the bank drive-through, the person who changes out the uniforms and rugs, the advertising person at our local paper or even the insurance agent.

Partnering businesses have an effect on our business. It is important that you make a point to build a relationship in some capacity with the people you interact with outside of "typical" customers. If you do this right, you will strengthen the structure and the awareness of your company in the community and with companion businesses that can benefit your business.

Keep in mind that the people you have a business relationship with have the potential to promote your business when they are working with their other customers and business partners. You have the power to use your customer service approach to ensure that they have a good opinion about you and your venture. You can almost look at this as a publicity opportunity. The people that you "do business with" can essentially become your unofficial sales and marketing department. Keep these key tactics in mind when building the relationships you have with people with whom you network.

- Be upbeat and positive
- Ask them about their day and how they have been
- Listen when they are talking and find common ground
- Be interested in what they are saying and ask questions
- Try to learn something new about them on a regular basis

Community involvement

As business owners, especially in small, tight-knit communities and in rural America, you probably already know the value of being involved in your community. Community involvement can be overlooked and is easy to negotiate off your plate. It is vitally important and therefore worth mentioning.

> ### *Rule of Thumb:*
> Being visible in your community often gives your customers another chance to get to know you and vice versa.

They will see you have a stake in your community's progress on both a personal and business level. No, you can't be involved in everything all the time, but joining one or two organizations you are passionate about will connect you to the community.

In the community that I live in, our local Culligan® water business is a great example of this type of involvement. Russ Specht (check out his *Rule of Thumb* book; *A Guide to Employee Relations*) is the owner of the franchise in Hastings, NE. He requires that his employees be involved in the community at least five hours per year and encourages more. He feels this is necessary for them to connect to their customers and give back. As the owner, he is involved in many local organizations from serving on the YMCA Board to Big Brothers and Big Sisters to even being active with an organization of small business owners, Hastings Entrepreneurs Group.

Another way for you to be involved and visible is to support the other small business owners in your community by being a patron of their establishments. Eat at their restaurants, subscribe to their services, and purchase your products and services from their stores. This will resonate with other business owners, as well as their customers.

Rule of Thumb:
It is vital that when you do business in the midlands and smaller communities that you support each other and share customer base.

It will make a good impression when your customers see you doing business in other small businesses and, yet again, it establishes a common ground.

Setting the bar by managing customer expectations

We have all been taught that life lesson: The only person we can control is ourselves! Well, in customer service, that rings true yet again. Business owners must be sure they are doing all that can be done to be proactive in business and creating an ideal platform for the development, growth and sustainability of customer expectations. Customer Expectation Management (CEM), a relatively new practical theory, is the ideal that requires companies to identify and clarify what can be expected by customers. The most important part of this business practice is that the businesses must meet these expectations without exception. The CEM practices quickly become part of the routine processes and will also become part of that experience for the customers.

When a company can meet the expectations of customers without faltering, the business will be impacted positively. The number of customers will increase, the retention-rate of customers will also stay steady and may even grow and the profit will increase. By setting the bar for the customers, you are taking control of the situation. You are letting them know what they can expect and over time, they will become very reliant on "knowing" what they will get when they do business with you. Customers want to be aware and certain about what they are going to purchase and experience. When they become satisfied by this and by the confidence they have doing business with you, they will begin to share this information with others. This is the best and strongest form of advertising that any business can get. As a society, we place a great deal of relevance on the recommendations of our friends, peers, co-workers and family. When someone that we trust advises us and suggests products and services to us, we listen and we usually give it a try.

On the same theory, you must let customers know when you are going beyond the expectations. If you are "treating" a customer to a special service like free delivery, sample products, or a discounted rate because of over-stock, then it is vital that you let them know this. If you don't tell them that you are doing something extra, they may become used to it and expect it each time. This sets the stage for disappointment. You don't want your customers to be disappointed because that will create a sense of negativity and dissatisfaction with the experience. Think of this as a time to give them a little extra. Explaining this to a customer might be a little tricky, but it is very important that you communicate to them that it is a one-time-only situation or for a special reason.

Example:

A coffee shop is trying out some new biscotti recipes over the week. They have an overabundance of biscotti so they plan to give each customer that orders a specialty drink a free biscotti cookie. If this is your first time in the coffee shop and you order a drink, you will get a free cookie. Unless someone tells you, you might think this is the normal practice. Then what happens the next time that you go in and you don't get a cookie? Will you wonder why? Will you ask the barista why you didn't get a free cookie? You can imagine the disappointment and potential awkward situation that this might create. However, when you purchase your drink, if you are told that because of new product recipes that are coming soon, you can get a FREE cookie this week! Or even better, the customers can just be told that they are getting a FREE cookie as a special token of appreciation for being such a great customer. However it is explained, it needs to be communicated. It is a good chance to do something extra for the customer, but be sure they know it is something *extra*. What would happen if the customer recommends the coffee shop to a friend and tells the friend that they get a free cookie? Imagine the disappointment if that friend does go and expects a cookie and doesn't get it. Not only will they feel short-changed, but they might also feel not as special of a customer as the person who suggested they do business there.

One of the foundations for ensuring that you are managing customer expectations in the best way possible is to have strong systems in place. When you create systems that have specific procedures that can be repeated time after time, you will begin to see similar outcomes each time. You want to identify what practices are successful and bring the most customers to your business as well as those that bring the most profitable results. Making those practices routine and part of the business system, your customers will develop expectations and the results will be beneficial to everyone. Some well-known companies who have done an excellent job creating systems and managing customer expectations include FedEx®, Apple®, Starbucks®, McDonalds® and Amazon®. When customers do business with these companies, they know what to expect and rarely do they get anything that is different than what they have become familiar with.

In summary, remember, you are your business. How you handle yourself outside of your establishment is as important as what you do while working in it. Engage everyone around you, especially your business partners and neighboring entrepreneurs. Be known by others in your community by getting involved. This is one of the best ways to raise awareness about your business, what you are doing, and it just makes you feel good! You control how you handle your business. You must be proactive to what customers expect by managing customer expectations through systems you have created and executed. Once you have built a following you must always deliver on what is expected. These efforts will impact your business and your customer relationships in a very positive way.

Chapter 5
Serving the Different Generations

This chapter started as a section in the previous chapter, but I think it needs a chapter dedicated to it because it is very significant for small businesses.

Rule of Thumb:
We have established that communication is key for performing excellent customer service.

It is very important to know that how you communicate with your customer effectively will be very dependent on the generation in which they belong. The information in this chapter is generalized. There will always be those individual cases where a person displays traits that are outside of the normal generational characteristics. However, it is a good practice to have a grasp on how to communicate to the generations. Each generation has different expectations when it comes to customer service.

A generation is defined by a group of people that are in the same age range that were raised in and live in about the same area geographically and experience the same life events. Generations can be divided up to the following categories:

- Matures – born between 1900 - 1945
- Baby Boomers – born between 1946 - 1964
- Generation X – born between 1965 - 1980
- Generation Y – born between 1981 - 1994
- Generation M – born between 1995 - 2000

Let's start first with some generalized traits for each group:

Matures (also known as the Silent Generation) – These folks were influenced by the Great Depression, WWII and Communism. Because of the strength of the military, this generation rose through the workplace fashioned in the command-style management that made them respect authority based on hierarchy and protocol. This generation is very practical, they have a dedicated work ethic and they show authority a great deal of respect. They believe in self-sacrifice and they are very conscience of money and value each penny that they earn.

Baby Boomers - They experienced the opposite of the generation before them as they grew up with unlimited opportunity. Television was a cultural experience as well as the Vietnam War, the needs of children and women, the sexual revolution and the Civil Rights movement. This generation is known for population density thus forcing the Boomers to compete in the workplace, which made them work very hard. This group was optimistic, and driven about doing good work. They began to challenge authority and they felt that what you do in your work defines who you are in life. They also treated money in a different way than their parents by spending more on non-essential things like recreational items such as boats, vacation homes, and elite automobiles.

Generation X (also known as Latchkey Kids) – This collection of people experienced the global economic erosion and saw how their parent's jobs were restructured. This led to social problems such as higher divorce rates, rising crime and unwed births. They were introduced to the personal computer and saw the fall of the Soviet Empire. The Gen-Xers, as they are often referred to, grew up to be very self-sufficient and independent because of both parents working outside of the home. They learned not to trust or rely on societal promises and that nothing is permanent. Generation X has a skeptical outlook and they consider themselves free-agents that don't respond well to micro-managing. They expect to be getting what they work for and want to be entitled to rights and privileges that they earn. This generation works for their lifestyle and have high expectations of those in leadership roles.

Generation Y (also known as Millenials) – This is the first generation that has been celebrated by their parents and extended family. They were raised by parents who over-compensated their own broken childhoods by showing praise and awarding them continuously. This generation has not had to face too many hardships in life and many of them continue to live at home with their parents into adulthood. This group feels that they are greatly appreciated by everyone around them. They have been raised in a technological era where cell phones, the Internet and instant communication all emerged. They were impacted by 9/11 and the war in Iraq. They tend to be fairly confident, but not great problem-solvers. They are uncertain how they feel toward authority and they do not differentiate work and life as they feel their work should reflect their lifestyle. This group is greatly influenced by their peers as they have the perception that everyone should be treated fairly. They do not value money as it has been something that they come by from their parents or by chance.

Generation M (for Multi-Tasking also known as Linksters) - This group is just entering the workforce, college and the business world. This is a group of young people that are more connected electronically and technologically than any other generation. They are less physically active than the prior two generations. However, they are mentally able to balance conversations and stimulations that are happening simultaneously. They are able to follow examples that they are shown, and this generation does not respond well to criticism. They have been told that anything is possible and that they are not at fault when things go wrong. This comes from the blame they have seen their parents put on teachers and government. They are used to being a part of a team and they are involved with highly scheduled activities. They were brought up in the age of safety overload. They do not think outside of the box very well and they tend to struggle with how to handle free-time. Their culture has taught them to crave attention and to be comfortable sharing private information about themselves. They have been impacted by social media and always having an electronic connection in some way and often more than one.

Rule of Thumb:
In order to serve people in your business it is helpful to consider the generation that your customers fit into.

Generational research shows that the Boomers and the Matures feel younger than their actual age. What is important is that the younger generations do not share this feeling and often perceive or treat the Boomers and Matures older than they feel. This can cause a great deal of animosity when it comes to customer service.

If you are working with a customer that is in a different generation than you are, you must consider the different values and expectations that they have. Someone who is a Mature or Boomer will be respectful of the fact that you need to double-check to be sure that you are authorized to complete something. They have a respect for authority and find value in hierarchy-structured management. They are also more cautious and believe in doing things the right way first. A Generation X customer might be bothered by this and feel that you lack leadership and decisiveness. Their generation questioned those in charge and learned to doubt leadership because of the failure they experienced in the economy and government.

The price of your product or service will have much more bearing on a customer who is in the Mature or Boomer group than someone from the Generation Y or Millennial group. Remember, the younger generations have not had to "plan" financially so they are often oblivious to negotiating prices. They assume that you would give them the best because they deserve the best. The tone of voice and positive praise that you use with a Gen-Yer or Millennial will be much more important to them than it would be to a customer from Generation X or a Boomer. The Gen-Xer or Boomer will base their experience on getting the best deal possible for the best price. The Gen-Yer or Millennial will base the experience on how important you make them feel in the transaction, especially if it is in front of their peers. Explaining the features and benefits to a Gen X customer is going to be very important. They want you to "prove" it to them and justify why they should make a purchase. Whereas someone from the Millennial and even some from the Gen Y group will just trust that you are giving them the product that they should use and wouldn't try to cheat them because you admire them and think you should have their best interests in mind.

Try to be aware of the generation of your target customer as well as the other customers that you encounter on a regular basis. Knowing some of these generational traits can help you deal with them in an effective way. Remember, these are simplified assumptions based on generational research and that each person is ultimately different. Ideally, you can assess each customer and customize your approach to meet their needs, but knowing some of the traits that come from specific groups of people will help you develop your customer service strategies.

Resources:

Johnson, L., & Johnson, M. (2010). Generations, Inc. New York, NY: American Management Association.

Exceptional Customer Service Across Generations: How to Harness
   the Power of Generational Dynamics to Drive Your Transit
   Organization Forward. (2010). National Rural Transit Assistance
   Program [Data file]. Retrieved from http://www.nationalrtap.org/
   LinkClick.aspx?fileticket=2cIfLeMiyNs%3D&tabid=1524

Defining Generations. (2009 – 2012) Retrieved from: http://www.
   generationaldiversity.com/index.php?/faq.html

Chapter 6
How can you have Excellent Customer Service?

The leading component of customer service

You are the customer service in your business.

Rule of Thumb:
As a small business owner, you are the one who sets the stage and executes on customer service.

In rural America, where small businesses exist and rely upon customer loyalty more than ever, customer service is the one thing that can determine your success. The best part about having an excellent customer service plan is that (in theory) it doesn't have to cost anything, but the value is priceless. That is very good return on investment!

I had to have oral surgery about ten years ago to remove two of my wisdom teeth, and it was not something I looked forward to at all. I knew that I had many different options in selecting a surgeon. My regular dentist recommended a few and my insurance provider also gave me some names. To be honest, I remember selecting the dentist that best fit my schedule. In my years, I have only found one person that actually enjoys going to the dentist, so I think most of us actually walk into the situation with our defenses up. Imagine having that hurdle to clear right at the start!

To my surprise, this experience turned out to be completely different than I had expected. I went in for the consultation, and I left feeling very comfortable and informed about everything I needed to do prior to and after surgery. I knew that I needed to have a ride home. I couldn't go back to work for a day, and my food choices had to be mild and soft. When I went in the morning for the surgery, they had me put on some headphones, dialed up my genre of music and away they went. After the surgery, my sister-in-law picked me up, swung by the grocery store deli to get me some mashed potatoes and gravy for later and delivered me safely at home to relax for the rest of the day to recover. I will never forget that in the middle of the afternoon my phone rang and it was the actual oral surgeon calling me. He told me that he wanted to be sure I was doing okay and to see if I had any questions.

Aside from having a mouth full of cotton and being under the influence of some really sedating pain medication, I felt as if I were experiencing a super-natural occurrence. The doctor…the actual surgeon who did my procedure was on the other end of the phone. He was just calling to make sure I was okay and to see how I was feeling? Really? Didn't he have other more pressing things to deal with? He didn't have one of the dental assistants or the office people call me instead? HE, the doctor, actually called me – I couldn't believe it. But yes, this really happened. I will never forget this experience, and it made me feel awesome. I don't know if that was a trick or something that dentists or oral surgeons learn in school, but I will tell you that it changed my entire perspective and I recommended that oral surgeon to EVERYONE that I knew and told EVERYONE about this experience. I had such a positive feeling because the surgeon thought that I was important enough that he called me. I think this even aided in my speedy recovery. The conversation lasted about two minutes at the most. I figured that it probably took him about five minutes to get my number, call and then to note the follow up and results in my record log.

So let's put this to the numbers and see how it adds up – if he did two surgeries per hour on average for about six hours per day that would be about 12 total. If he spent 5 minutes contacting each patient, that would result in about one hour of follow-up time each day. How wise is this on his part? If each patient had a similar response to mine, I would say this is well worth the effort and the time.

Rule of Thumb:
Under-Promise and Over-Deliver

This is the perfect example of the "under-promise, over-deliver" concept. I did recall being told that someone would be calling to check up on me within a few days. That was the under promise. I certainly wasn't expecting to be called so soon or for the doctor to call himself. That was the over deliver. Consider the situation if I had been told that the doctor would be calling me that afternoon to check in and it never happened? I would be disappointed which would have left me with a feeling of neglect.

If you have any doubt about delivering on a promise that you make to a customer, DO NOT MAKE IT. This is critical. If you disappoint your customers, they will always have that leverage and will think less of you. That doesn't mean that you can't make a commitment or obligate yourself, but be aware of the unexpected and account for it.

The majority of the time you will be able to meet the goal and succeed in the eyes of your customer, but the one time that you fall short will certainly carry a lot of weight. Instead, allow for the margin with the unexpected and this practice will work to your benefit nine out of ten times. If you know that shipping a product in the state takes three days, be sure to tell the customer that it should arrive within four to five days. You will be a superstar because most of the time the customer will receive their product early but in case it does take the full amount of time the customer will not be disappointed.

Equipping your team

Although you may start your business and be the only one at the helm in the beginning, you still have to think about your customer service strategy in terms of a team. Whether you do have employees or you are working with partners and maybe even independent contractors, these people all contribute to your team.

 Rule of Thumb:
It is important that you choose the right people to be on your team.

If another person has anything to do with your business, they should be considered part of your team. They represent your company in some fashion, and you want to be sure that they have the talents, skills and tools to do the best job possible. To do this, consider the steps below:

Step 1 - Choose the right people

As we have established in the previous chapters, one of the first steps to remarkable customer service is communication. You can teach a member of your team about a product, how to take inventory, how to wire an electrical box or even rebuild a computer; but you can't teach them how to be comfortable and friendly. These are adaptive skills that in most cases come naturally or have been established over a long period of time because of the person's upbringing, experiences and influences. Adaptive skills help people adjust to different situations easily. As cliché as it sounds; you either have it or you don't. If being outgoing, listening well and problem solving are not skills of the team member; chances are it never will be.

Rule of Thumb:
As the leader, you need to be sure that you are putting the right people in the right positions.

If you have someone who deals directly with the customer, you need to be sure that person is good at this. If they aren't, it could lead to the demise of something you have spent a great deal of time and effort building.

Step 2 – Lead by Example

This has never been more important than it is right now with the Generation Y and the Milliennials entering the workforce. These younger folks have been raised, by my generation, in a way that has not been conducive to thinking outside of the box. This generation has been directed and shown exactly what to do and how to do it. However, I have found that once they are shown what to do and they have it down, they excel in their role. Therefore, if you have team members that maybe need a little guidance and nudging this could be your opportunity. Encourage them to watch you when you deal directly one-on-one with a customer issue. Work the sales floor with these team members so that they can see you in action. The likelihood that they will replicate your actions and procedures is very high. They will see that this works and get the job done. You can even take this a step further and role-play with your team. You will be surprised how you can re-create situations and then discuss different outcomes based on different strategies. If you want your team to be able to handle difficult situations and become creative, you must show them what you have done to be successful. This, in a sense, gives them permission to follow the example and to also be successful.

Step 3 – Recognize, Reward and Show Appreciation

Rule of Thumb:
The younger workforce is driven by recognition and awards so it has never been as important to have a systems in place to acknowledge your team when they succeed.

They like to get attention when they are doing a good job, and they like everyone around them to know as well. It might seem unnecessary, but we have created this situation. Now we have to make it work. Keep in mind that this is generalized information and not everyone fits this description. The more experienced generations are typically satisfied with their superior appreciating their hard work. Just hearing a simple, "Thanks for taking care of that customer so well" is enough to let them know they did well. Identify reward or recognition methods that will actually mean something to the person you are dealing with.

Step 4 – Allow Leaders to Emerge

Business owners tend to crave control and want to be considered the leaders. This is by nature one of the things that make good entrepreneurs. They can feel a sense of caution when empowering their team to take on leadership roles because they are hesitant to relinquish power. In actuality, this is a sign of growth not only as an entrepreneur, but as a person. This gets you one step closer

to the top of that hierarchy of needs that Maslow created;
mentioned earlier. When a team member or a person who
you consider a partner or contributor to your business steps
up and delivers on customer service in a way that makes
a difference, stand back and let it happen. They may not
perform the same way you would in the given situation, but
this is how they learn.

Rule of Thumb:
Giving ownership to a team member will boost
their confidence to handle customer situations.

This is where the magic happens. Another way to deal
with the success is to encourage other team members to
acknowledge the method it was handled and to recognize
it. Often, peer-review or praise will have an even greater
impact.

Step 5 – Don't be the scapegoat

How many times have you been in a situation where an
employee says to you, "well, I can check with my boss" or
"we are not allowed to do that" or "I don't know if we can
give you a discount." Be sure that you have systems in place
to enable team members that interact with the customers to
deliver on service. If they are cut off from making decisions
when faced with a challenge or consumer question, it will
create a moment of doubt for them and for the customer.

You want to create an environment that doesn't make you look like the almighty OZ or a mean ogre that everyone is afraid of upsetting. If your employees feel that they can't fulfill the request of a customer because they lack the authority or the proper tools to do so, your customer will lose trust in your team and ultimately your leadership. You don't want to make that kind of impression. Think about it this way: A customer contacts your car rental business, and a team member answers the phone. The customer complains because the car they rented had a broken stereo. The customer wants to be credited or compensated in some way because this was not to his liking. Which response sounds better?

RESPONSE #1 – "I am very sorry, sir. I will check with the owner and see if he will allow us to do anything about this."

RESPONSE #2 – "I am very sorry, sir. I can understand how that would be frustrating for you since you were driving a long distance. My goal is to make sure you are happy. I will certainly reimburse you for this inconvenience. Our policy is to give you 50% of the rental fee as a credit. Is this satisfactory?"

The first response puts all the pressure on the "boss" or the owner. It is demeaning for the employee. It sends the message to the customer that keeping the owner happy is more important to the employee than keeping the customer happy. My opinion is that it also negates the employee's ability to serve as a sales associate…if they don't have any power to fix a problem, why would a customer respect their opinion or position when the employee is trying to sell them something?

The second response creates the image for the customer that the employee is equipped to handle the situation and that the company has its business in order with a policy in place.

Customer Promise

Instead of creating a guarantee or sharing your mission statement with your customers, why not do something more personal?

> **Rule of Thumb:**
> A customer promise is your own way of proclaiming your devotion to making your customers happy.

Often a promise adds more of an individualized focus to what is being assured.

Here is an example:

Customer Promise - *Our Promise to you…ask listen solve.*

They are not just words. They're our way of doing business. We ask *about your needs, the ways you like to do things, your financial* goals. And we **listen**. *Closely, and not because we're nosey. And, not because we want to "sell" you something. But because in order to* *solve, we must understand your banking needs and sometimes even your life needs. Only then can we help find personalized solutions for you. At Commerce, it's our promise to you.* ask listen solve.

(www.commercebank.com)

Customer Promise - *You ask, we listen!*

With our services we are striving to make your life easier and easier every day. Simplifying doesn't mean cutting corners - on the contrary, simplified services translate into increased accessibility and usability for our clients.

Reliable, high quality, scalable and transferable – this is how our sustainable solutions are built. Combined with a comprehensive understanding of the current and future needs of our customers we create the basis for long-term partnerships.

DHL (http://www.dhl-brandworld.com/en/our-mission/customer-promise.html)

A customer promise is an innovative method to let the customer know the importance of what you are saying. Tradition has taught us that breaking a promise has a negative connotation. We lose our credibility, we disappoint others and we hurt our reputation. Based on that, by calling it a promise we take it more seriously. This caveat might be the most important aspect of the customer promise.

Rule of Thumb:
A customer promise can add that personal touch to online businesses and websites where there is less opportunity to provide that connection with customers.

If your business is strictly Internet or electronic commerce or you have a strong online presence, you may want to consider making the customer promise very visible on your website. It is a good way to "personalize" that experience for them.

Give them something extra

An effective customer service strategy is to think small but unique. Growing up in my small home town, I remember a police officer who always carried packs of Double-Mint or Big Red gum with him. When a kid in the community would come up to him, he would give them a stick of gum. This created a very comfortable way for younger children to get acquainted with him. He went onto become successful with the force as he made a positive connection with the community. You can do the same type of thing in your business.

Rule of Thumb:
Give your customers something unique and special that they can only expect from you.

If you own a retail business, have catchy jokes printed on the back of your receipts. Give out a "free" cup of coffee card to each customer to encourage them to go down the street to another small business. If you have an online business, email your customer a free music download, a free quote of the day, or the link to a podcast that you think is generally valuable. Be consistent with your "something extra," and point out your extra offering in the beginning so the customer realizes the added value they are receiving. Even though this is a small gesture, it can have big impact and certainly sets you apart from the rest.

Take it a step further

It is amazing how much the little things can make such a big difference. It might take a little more effort and some additional thought, but having excellent customer service will be worth it in the long run. It kind of goes back to the lesson we were taught with the Golden Rule – in this same spirit, give your customers the level of service that you would like to receive.

In fact, if you do that and add a little extra, you know you have this in the bag.

Rule of Thumb:
When given the chance to come through and deliver good customer service, ask yourself the question of how you can take your service a step further.

For example, help your customer solve a problem that goes beyond the parameters of your business. I observed this situation when visiting a mobile phone service provider's retail store. A customer had just purchased a new phone and needed a protective case. The customer wanted a specific case, but the store did not carry that type.

The representative told her that she could get this cover at a larger electronics store that was a few blocks away. He then took it a step further and called the other store to check that they had the case in stock that the customer wanted. I was so impressed by what I witnessed. I let two other customers go before me in the service line just so that when it was my turn, I could have this GREAT customer service representative help me. I also made sure that I mentioned this to him so that he knew how awesome he was for giving this level of service.

Measure your customer service

It is important to know what your customer base expects of your business. Dena Beck, a Business Specialist with the Center for Rural Development in Nebraska, shared a great exercise with me. I actually put this to use when meeting with small business owners in my area. Each person wrote down their business name with an explanation if needed. Then the cards were shuffled and distributed to the group. Each person got a card with a different business name on it. They then had to list three things that they felt would demonstrate _good_ customer service. Then the cards were shuffled again and redistributed. Each person had a card that was not their own business. They had to write three things they would expect from this business in regard to _excellent_ customer service. The group then gave each business their original card back and each business shared what was written. Many of the business owners learned things they had not even thought about as being part of the service offering in their business. This activity had lasting effects and was very helpful to entrepreneurs in a comfortable setting.

This was a good exercise within this group as it allowed the entrepreneurs to learn what was expected from their business through a different perspective. The lesson you can take from this is to ask others what they think. We see big businesses enticing customers with discounts and special deals if they fill out a survey that helps them rate their experience. Bonuses, paychecks, product lines, plan-o-grams, and other important decisions are made in the corporate world based on these survey results. These types of surveys aren't seen as much in the world of small business. They might be impersonal, but they ask important questions. Business owners often don't ask because they fear what they might learn. They fear that the feedback might be different than what they want to hear.

 Rule of Thumb:
You can't ignore the truth.

You can't avoid a potential learning situation just because you are afraid of how it will make you feel. You must face the situation head on in your business so that you can deal with it, learn from it and improve upon it. The longer you avoid addressing issues and expectations, the longer you are giving the concern to grow and bad habits to form. It can become problematic and potentially damaging to your business. Ask your customers what they want, what they expect and how you can make your business better. Remember as we discussed earlier, the customer is the life-blood of your business and their opinion should matter to you.

Eventually, you will want to measure your customers' satisfaction of your service. Many Customer Relationship Management (CRM) programs are already integrated with measurement features. If you aren't already working with a system that does this, there are several separate software options you can purchase or create your own. You can also request the service of secret shoppers or other agencies that are focused on this type of service. Regardless of how you chose to measure your customer service, be sure to stick with it over a period of time or even indefinitely. You want to be able to track this information to gauge your progress.

When developing best practices on delivering excellent customer service, keep in mind the concept of "under-promise and over-deliver." Be sure to set examples with your employees, business partners and even other customers on how to execute good customer service. Recognize and empower those around you when they are excelling at any component of their job, but especially when they bring good service to a customer. Consider making your efforts more personable by creating and sharing your customer promise. Give your customers something extra by going the extra step that might make a difference in their experience. It is important to measure the business's growth when it comes to customer service.

Chapter 7
Client-Based Businesses

We have established that there are many different types of
customers in your business. Many businesses deal with what is
often referred to as clients. Clients are customers who also carry
with them a different perspective of your business. In a lot of cases,
they have different expectations from you and your business. To
define a client, consider this explanation: A client is someone who
consistently utilizes a professional service that your business offers.
Often a client is dependent on you for a specific function in their life.
You want to "protect" a client because they have more of a long-term
commitment to your services.

Although the difference may seem slight, it is significant and it
needs to be mentioned. Client and customer expectations will be
different, so you need to know how to handle each effectively. The
relationship that is built in a client-based business is very important.
Client-based businesses include doctors, counselors, insurance
agents, hair stylists, massage therapists, marketing agencies,
accounting firms, the veterinarians, real estate and even Internet
providers. Basically, any business that relies on regularly scheduled
or long-term customers who will remain loyal to offered services
should be considered a client-based business.

Even though businesses usually establish long-term relationships with clients, it is very important to keep in mind that these customers have choices too. Creating relationships that foster customer loyalty is critical for small business owners with a client base. Planning is essential in small business and knowing what income you can make and count on is important.

Rule of Thumb:
Having clients allows a business to anticipate monthly revenues and know how much income to expect.

Therefore, it is very important to keep your clients happy.

Everything that has been discussed in this book applies to client service. However, some of the factors that have an even more profound effect on the success of a client-based business include reputation, communication, and relationship.

Committed clients associate with business owners they trust. It is in your best interests to be this type of business. Clients don't always view the relationship as business and tend to make more personal choices. This is especially true when the interaction is reoccurring and they know they will continually do business with you. When a customer looks at sharing personal and confidential information, they want to be sure that the person they are giving this information to is someone that makes them feel comfortable. Your reputation will be very important because people will not feel good sharing with you if you are cold or evasive when discussing their needs. They will eventually do business elsewhere. Losing that customer's business is bad, but losing their recommendation to potential customers is worse.

Rule of Thumb:
Client-based businesses thrive and grow based on client loyalty and recommendations.

Communication is going to be even more paramount in a client-based business. A good guideline to follow is that you should touch base or communicate in some capacity with your client three-to-one (3:1). This means if your customer visits your business for some type of scheduled appointment (e.g. massage, oil-change), you should be communicating with them at least three times outside of that scheduled appointment. The same goes for payments. If you are paid for a service on a regular monthly basis, such as Internet service, insurance or security, you still need to take the time to communicate in some way to your customers. It is very important that you stay in their minds and let them know that you are there if they need anything "extra" or have questions.

If you are not staying connected with them in some way, it is much easier to stop doing business with you and choose another business. People like attention and they like acknowledgment when they are paying you. It doesn't mean that you have to make phone calls or personally visit each customer 3:1, but you do need to do something that will raise awareness that you are thinking of them, you appreciate them and you are available if needed. An email, a text, a postcard, or even posting a quick message on their Facebook wall are all ways of communication that reach clients.

How you communicate is just as important as the frequency.

> ### *Rule of Thumb:*
> Positive communication is essential when you are in the midst of a "deal" with a customer or client.

This includes developing a website, selling or buying a home, or helping them prepare taxes. More of these types of situations present themselves for businesses that are B2B enterprises. You know your business better than anyone else. Sometimes we don't always communicate in ways that allow our customers to fully understand how things work, but we don't recognize this disconnect. Many things can get lost in translation so it is essential to keep that in mind and to be patient with your clients. If you expect your clients to complete something by a deadline that will ensure your ability to complete the task, you need to communicate this and work in a reserve or grace period for them.

You need to allow for the unexpected and when things don't go as planned, you must be very careful to not blame your client. If you blame them or if they feel that they dropped the ball, they will be left with a negative feeling. As humans, we typically shy away from things that make us feel bad about ourselves. This can be difficult. This can often be one of the most frustrating things for a client-based business owner to do.

> ### Rule of Thumb:
> Sometimes, you just have to step back, realign
> the focus and move forward in a positive manner.

This is also something that you will be able to plan for as you get to know your clients better. For instance, my hair stylist knows that she needs to tell me my appointment is fifteen minutes earlier than it really is. This ensures that I get there in plenty of time and I don't waste hers, thus not making anyone feel bad or disappointed about the interaction.

Consider the following scenario:

A commercial landscaping company is preparing for the spring season. They have contacted clients to see who will be needing services for the season. They sent out an email and did follow-up calls to schedule regular appointments and to learn of special projects. There was a sign-up deadline. A customer who owns an office building is one of the clients. However, he didn't get back to the landscaping business by the deadline and his selected day for landscaping is not available.

CUSTOMER: *Yeah, we want you guys to do our lawn and take care of the bushes and stuff again this year. We want you to do this on Fridays, like last year.*

LANDSCAPING BIZ: *Oh, well, you didn't get back to us soon enough. We can't do it on Friday now. We sent out a card and also called you over a month ago, but you didn't let us know what was going on.*

How will the customer feel in this situation? Could it be handled differently?

CUSTOMER: *Yeah, we want you guys to do our lawn and take care of the bushes and stuff again this year. We want you to do this on Fridays, like last year.*

LANDSCAPING BIZ: *Great! You guys must be busy this season. We are booked up for Fridays, but I can put you on the list in case something changes. I apologize that Fridays are already filled up. We know you are busy in the beginning of the week, and that is why it works best for you toward the end. I want to make sure I get you put on our schedule so we have a time reserved. Would Thursday afternoons work for you?*

The tone of the second example is much different and the customer is more inclined to reconsider the time because the business owner is recognizing the needs of the client and focusing on how to make it work instead of "scolding" the client for not meeting the deadline. Note in the second take of the landscaping scenario, all of the words are positive, even though the response isn't giving the customer exactly what they want.   If the customer feels as if they have failed at something or didn't meet an expectation, they will have a negative inclination.

 Rule of Thumb:
It is important to deal with the interests rather than the positions.

If you keep your client's best interests in mind and let them know that, they tend to want to work with you and not change that routine. However, if you make them feel bad about a situation based on your position versus their position, the client may get defensive. This may be negative enough to make them reconsider their choice to do business with you.

The relationship you build with a client is of the utmost value to your business. This should also be valuable to you as a person. When you feel a special connection to another person, you tend to want to see great things happen for them.

Rule of Thumb:
You feel satisfaction when your customers are pleased with a service or the end result.

It is easy to try to separate the two worlds, but at the end of the day, it really isn't possible. One trait of an entrepreneur is a passion for what they are doing. This cannot be boxed or divided. Having good and positive relationships with your clients will add to that passion and allow your business to grow.

Keep in mind the scene in the movie *Jerry Maguire (1996)* where the agent hugs his client and another athlete sees this and feels very inferior because his agent doesn't treat him this way. Although that is a funny scene in a fictional movie, it is a very real example of how clients feel. They feel that they have a vested interest in your business because they selected you. They choose to do business with you. When they feel that they are bringing you a sense of satisfaction, this will in turn create that feeling for them.

Rule of Thumb:
Let your clients know that you appreciate them and that you value that relationship.

This doesn't mean that you have to go around hugging everyone, but find a way that works in your business and for your clients and go with it.

Clients differ from customers in that they have a longer-term commitment to your business and feel a sense of protection and service from you. It is very important to build a good reputation by being honest and fair in a client-based business. Communication is key to stay connected with clients. Be sure that this is consistent and ongoing. When you communicate with clients, it is vital that you always take on the blame and don't shift this to fall on the customer as they will feel negative about the situation. Build great relationships with your clients and eventually they will find more value in you than just the service you are offering because you make them feel good.

Chapter 8
Now what? How to Keep the Momentum Going

Customer Relationship Management (CRM)

You have identified your target market. You have communicated to them and other potential customers. You have grown your customer base and improved your customer service by equipping yourself, your team, and your business with all the necessary tools. What comes next? It is now time for you to maintain the customer relationships that you have diligently created. This may be the most important part yet.

Fostering relationships is very important if you want your customers to keep thinking about your business, talking about your business and returning to your business.

> **Rule of Thumb:**
> You must consistently keep the lines of communication open.

You can communicate through emails, mobile marketing, direct mail coupons, referral programs, online surveys and many other message portals; but it has to be continuous.

To make this happen, you must collect data from each customer. This data should include a name, address, phone number, cell number, email address and anything else that is specific to your business like product or service of choice. Make notes about each encounter with the customer. Add information that they share and that you learn so that you can be successful at finding common ground and meeting their needs.

In choosing a CRM program or software package, it is important to research which option will best suit your business. As you decide how to track your customers, be sure that you are manually keeping the information somewhere even if it is just on index cards, the contact list in your phone, or even a notebook.

As you decide what program or system to go with, you must also consider the other infrastructures you use in your business like your accounting system and your point-of-sale (POS) system. Computerized programs like Quickbooks™ or GratisPOS by Agilx have a CRM that allows you to capture your customer data. Constant Contact® is another online service that allows small business owners to build a central hub of consumer information for communication purposes. Be sure that you are doing this as efficiently as possible to integrate with the system you are using. You don't want to waste time by entering data more than once if possible.

Social media

Due to the influx of social media stimulation for small businesses, we have seen many traditional methods of customer service go by the wayside. This is because small business owners feel that they have to shift the focus of follow-up in order to meet the needs of their customers through Facebook, Twitter, blogging and the like. Although it is good and highly recommended to have this online presence, it cannot be used to replace the traditional customer service methods.

Rule of Thumb:
You still need to actually talk to your customers.

You can't expect your customers to be as satisfied by your general status updates on your social media page as they were when you had made personal contact with them.

Yes, it does take more time, it does take more thought and it creates more work in many cases; but it will set you apart from the other competitors who now rely solely on social media. A small business, particularly in the midlands, will be expected to embody our Midwest values; good handshake, great eye contact, confidence in what we do, pride in our work and manners. You must keep these values in the recipe you create for customer service. So don't abandon the practices used in the past, but keep building these and mingle them with those that social media has to offer.

Business owners in this geographical area have to juggle keeping up with new technology without abandoning our core-value practices. Depending on your exact product and service and your target customer, your public will be expecting you to be responsive to technology. If you don't have a good website, if you don't have a Facebook page for your business, if you don't text customers when there is a sale, they may think that you're behind the times or non-responsive not only with technology but with the products and services that you offer. You want to avoid this.

Rule of Thumb:
You want to show your customers that you are on the leading edge in your offerings and communication methods.

Taking advantage of the many opportunities social media offers will put you ahead of the curve. The biggest thing to remember is to be consistent. If you post your menu each day on your Facebook page, make sure to do it at the same time and in the same format each day to create consistency for your customers. If you blog about your business or industry, be sure to post your blogs on a regular basis. You also need to be offering information in your blogs that is helpful and informative to your customer audience. This is an opportunity to "give" them something valuable and to gather their feedback. If they respond by posting a comment or a question, be sure to acknowledge them.

Rule of Thumb:
Customers who are engaged in social media do so because they thrive on the "instant" element that it provides.

They want to see immediate responses.

When was the last time that you ordered something online and had the company follow-up with a personal phone call to thank you? Would this be impactful? I am still impressed when I get a handwritten thank you note in the mail after a purchase. It shows that the business does care and does appreciate that I am their customer. Can you think of ways that you can effectively use social media but still be responsive to customers in a personable way? It may take more effort, but it may be just the thing that makes your customer choose to do business with you over the competition when they are presented with a choice in the future.

No Response will usually result in No Business

Regardless of how you communicate with your customers and how you continue to raise awareness of your business, you must be consistent. You must also be reliable. One of the biggest mistakes that a business can make is to not respond to a customer. If a customer has called, emailed or even texted you…be sure to respond. If you don't do this in a timely fashion or at all, you are at risk of losing that customer. People do not like to be ignored. When there is not a response, this is usually the feeling evoked. Even if you set a specific time of day to respond to customer issues, questions or concerns, be sure to do this. If your customer is very eager to hear from you, but you haven't solved their problem, let them know you are working on it. Do not chance the negative impact that might occur by simply not responding. Customers will appreciate that you are taking care of them and that their issue is as important to you as it is to them.

Gathering customer data is one of the primary things you will need to do on a regular basis for your small business. Knowing your customers and communicating with them through traditional channels as well as social media prospecting will be vital. Set aside ample time to do this and put in the effort that is necessary so this process is efficient.

Chapter 9
Creating a Unique Business Model

Create a culture and something that makes a difference for a customer. Customers have unlimited choices when it comes to products and available services. In order to create a demand in the market for your business, you will have to create an experience for the customer. Never before have businesses been as consumer driven as they are with the current competitive economy. If your business succeeds, it will certainly be due to the popularity and positive response by your consumers. People trust their friends, neighbors, and coworkers. When someone in their "circle" recommends something, they listen and they typically act on it. Make the experience of doing business with your company one that people talk about and tell others about.

Doug Bruce was mentioned in an earlier chapter. He is a local business owner in Hastings, NE, and has restructured his organization. He no longer calls the employees that sell salespeople. He now refers to them as problem-solvers. Customers don't just magically appear at the door step.

Rule of Thumb:
The reason customers are doing business is to find a solution to a problem they are facing.

When you can identify that challenge, relate to it, and offer options and potential resolutions, you are delivering on customer service.

This is not revolutionary. However, doing this in a way that is memorable, unique and beyond the customer's expectations is something worth trying. We base our expectations on what we know and how things have happened in the past. We don't always deal well with situations that are unfamiliar to us and often because of that we bow out of opportunities that could turn out to be remarkable.

In order to compete and be successful, something to consider is creating a business model that is unique and innovative. How you bring your products and services to your customers could very well set you apart from the competition.

As we examine high-growth companies and businesses that have received a great deal of publicity and awareness, one thing that most of them have in common are distinctive business models. They deliver in a way that gives them the competitive advantage.

One local company in Nebraska that I have had the pleasure of learning about is Energy Pioneer Solutions. This company is only three-years-old and they have grown at an incredible rate. They are an energy company. Through usage analysis and energy assessments, they can diagnose the energy and comfort needs of the home, fix them, finance them and monitor them with very little help from the home or business owner. Energy Pioneer Solutions has streamlined this process so that it causes as little disruption to the customer as possible, but saves them money. They determine upgrades, repairs and improvements that can be made to the structure that will save energy and reduce the amount of money being paid for monthly utilities. The price for the improvements is recovered over a period of time based on the amount of money saved by the customer on the actual utility bill. Here is how it works: If a customer's utility bill is $300 per month before the service and is reduced by $100 each month after the service both parties win! Of that $100 savings, the customer gets $50 and Energy Pioneer Solutions gets $50 for the next five years. After five years, the entire savings amount belongs to the customer. The customer has a more efficient home, often upgraded equipment and with a higher market value.

Typically, in order for a business to make more money, a customer has to spend more money. That is the revenue model that we are taught and the expected method for a business to be profitable. However, in the case of Energy Pioneer Solutions, they have created a very different model where the more money they save a customer, the more money they make. Their model is designed and works for all income levels. This unique business model has proven to be successful for the company and has allowed them to grow quickly and gain the attention of other states and communities who are eager to bring Energy Pioneer to their areas to implement this concept and service.

Another company that has created a new business model that has caught on in a big way is TOMS Shoe Company, founded by Blake Mycoskie in 2006. The creative way that TOMS has seen so much success is because of the social responsibility that it has integrated into the business process. Mycoskie created the One for One™ business approach. For each pair of shoes purchased by a customer, a pair of shoes is given to a child in need of shoes.

Philanthropy is always a welcomed act and typically we see successful entrepreneurs give back to the world when they become wealthy and prosperous. That is what we expect to see with social responsibility. However, with TOMS, the philanthropy is put into the hands of the customer at the time of purchase. When I walk around in my TOMS shoes, I find it satisfying to know that I provided a child in need with a pair of shoes, and that everyone who sees my shoes will know that I did this as well. This is a brilliant strategy to have a business model that makes a profit, but also serves a greater purpose.

Responding to competition with an approach that offers a different perspective to a customer is a challenge. The trick is to find a niche or a unique way to meets the customer's needs, especially if you are in a field that has very "traditional" ways of doing business. Tim and Hillarie Redline, of Hastings, NE started their own pharmacy in the rural city in which I live. Currently, there are about thirteen different pharmacies in our small community. How could they possibly be successful as a new business with this type of competition? Redline Pharmacy is servicing customers' medication needs in distinct ways that are new and not being offered by the competition. They are doing this because they saw the need with patients and wanted to create a different path for consumers to obtain prescription medication. They specialize in compounding customized medications, home infusion services and hormone replacement therapy. These are three different and specialized services that make their business model unique. Redline Pharmacy is approaching its tenth anniversary and currently employs about ten people in the community. They have ventured into public education about health issues and been able to compete very well by being innovative in their product and service offerings.

Rule of Thumb:
Think about your business and how you can appeal to your customers in a different way that brings value to them and the community that you serve.

What can you do that will be different than what is expected by your customers and what is normal for your industry? Is it possible that you can make your customer part of a new and exciting movement? If you develop a business model that is leading edge and creative, can you involve your customer in the process? It is very possible that if they are involved with something new, significant and leading edge, they will feel more committed to your company. This is the type of customer service that will support those happy, repeat customers.

Chapter 10
Make your Customer your Super Hero

It's a bird. It's a plane. It's your customer. Business owners are often bogged down on a daily basis with all of the tasks, processes and logistics of running the business. When you make your to-do list each day, rarely will you add: <u>get to know my customer better</u>, <u>try to bring value to my customers</u>, <u>tell my customers how great they are</u>, or even <u>thank my customers</u>. These are those things that are taken for granted by both the business owner and the customers. We just assume that these practices are part of the daily routine. But, what happens when they aren't?

You can have the most unique product or service. The window of your retail store may be very cool and visually appealing. You might have one of the most technologically advanced point-of-sale systems. You may offer over 500 different types of widgets. You may have some of the best industry training in your trade. If you don't have any customers, is any of it worth anything?

> **Rule of Thumb:**
> Each day you must realize what the customer brings to your business, and ultimately that is profit.

Your customer is what makes it possible for you to carry the unique goods and offer the specialized services. The customer is how you afford to upgrade that POS system to be more effective. The profit you gain from your customers' business is how you afford to continue learning about and growing in your industry. The profit you make will allow you to have up-to-date and great looking displays. The customer is the super hero of your business and if you don't have daily tasks that address that significance in your business, ultimately you will fail. Don't do that. Put your best foot forward and accept the fact that the customer's role in your business is that of a super hero. When you think about Wonder Woman, Superman, Captain America, or The Incredible Hulk, ask yourself how these figures serve as "super heroes."

They seem like ordinary people in the daily scheme of things. These figures are often outcasts or misunderstood in the societies they live in. Then necessity calls, the distress signal is used and they become the saving grace of those around them. When the chips are down and the well-being of your business is at stake, you need to know that you can count on your customers to be your super heroes. They can't do that without your belief in them. If you truly believe that your customers have the power that they really have, you will find value in them and they will know this. When they know this, they want to be that super hero for your business.

Think about this in terms of one of your favorite super heroes. In most of the "fictional" stories we are familiar with, the hero is always attracted to or works on behalf of at least one character that they know believes in the super hero's abilities although others my doubt them. They want to protect and serve that person beyond all obstacles. If you treat your customer with that same belief, that they have extraordinary powers in your business, they will in turn want to fulfill that role and be your super hero.

So, be sure as you truck along in the daily routine of your business, when you make your list of tasks to accomplish, you include the following:

- Learn more about my customers so I can help them better
- Make my customers know how much I appreciate them
- Let my customers see how much value they bring to my business
- Make each customer feel like a Super Hero!

Best Practices:

1. Develop a customer recognition program – remember to be consistent with this.

2. Ask customers why they do business with you. Do this on a regular basis.

3. Try a new communication approach and measure the results.

4. Become a member of an organization in your local community.

5. Offer a discount to certain organizations or a percentage of proceeds to that organization on a special day. Then partner with the organization to advertise that collaboration.

6. Have an advisory board that includes a person from each generation.

7. Challenge yourself to learn each customer's name and something new about them each time you interact with them.

8. Send out a personal thank you note each week to at least one customer. Make this specific.

9. Whenever a client is "news worthy" be sure to cut out the article and send it to them with a nice note.

10. Begin to gather the emails of your clients/customers. Set up a regularly scheduled time to either email them, blog about your industry or update your business facebook page.

11. Find a business similar to yours in a different location and visit or contact this business. Make note of something different they do and consider adapting it to work in your business.

12. Draw a map or flow chart of how you handle customer concerns in your business.

13. Encourage your customers to try other companion businesses. Sometimes you can even partner to offer mutual discounts.

14. Keep record of the most up-to-date sales and pricing structures of your competitors. Offer this information to your customers when they are curious about the competition.

15. Stay up on the most recent product and service advances in your industry.

16. Create an online FAQ (frequently asked questions) for your customers to learn more information.

17. Make a goal of calling back customers who were dealing with a problem. Follow-up to see how the solution is working.

18. Offer to sponsor a club that includes many of your customers. Maybe it can even be an interest club that involves your business industry (i.e. book store – start a writing club or a book club).

19. Create a new program that offers easy pay options like subscriptions or regular payments through bank drafts.

20. Ask customers to participate in giving advice to other customers. This could be done through written or recorded testimonials or just offering a phone number to call.

21. Create an incentive or reward program for your customers/clients.

22. Try to use less negative and more positive word choices. For example, instead of saying "That won't work," rephrase and say,"Let's visit more about how we can handle that challenge."

23. Write a customer promise and post it for customers to see; website, in your business, on business cards, newsletter... etc.

24. Keep a customer service journal and ask this of your staff. By logging in the experiences, you can look back through them to determine what was successful and what could be improved.

25. Implement an "honesty policy" for your business. Remember, customers have to trust people that they buy from, if they ever doubt that you are being truthful with them, they will not be return customers.

26. Have a FUN culture for your business. People are drawn to others who are HAPPY.

27. Keep interactive tracking tools in your business. This might be a map on the wall with a stick pin of each customer's address or a fun photo of a client when they get their hair done, and post it on your website and link it to their online social sites.

28. Observe the customer service you see all around you. Be sure to learn from each experience. Maybe even keep a record of these experiences.

29. Make a Feature and Benefit card for each product or service that is offered in your business. Keep these accessible for customers.

30. Join a group of other small business owners in your community and share best practices! If one doesn't exist – CREATE IT!!!

Good Luck!

Author Biography

As a guru of ideas and "out-of-the-box" thinking, Lisa has a vast experience of strategizing with existing businesses as well as new business owners. Her education, a BA in Organizational Communication and a Master's Degree in Organizational Management & Entrepreneurship, have proven to be a great foundation that has enabled her to bring the traditional best practices to companies while giving a new perspective with leading edge techniques. She has managed teams of people and been an award-winning salesperson. Lisa has also owned several of her own companies.

Her background is very diverse with work experience in many industries; energy, telecommunications, information technology, retail, marketing/advertising, media production, construction building and manufacturing. In addition to being the owner of Dynamic Concepts, Lisa is an Instructor of Entrepreneurship and Business at Central Community College and coordinates the Entrepreneurship Center at Central Community College. She is well versed in communication theory as well as applicable methods. She does several speaking events in the Midwest each year. She has authored books, articles and worked on many research projects.

She volunteers on local and state coalitions and boards. She is very active in her community and has lead several projects that have benefited business owners, non-profit organizations and education. Tschauner lives in central Nebraska with her husband, and two teenage children. She and her family enjoy traveling, art, riding motorcycles and restoring their old home.